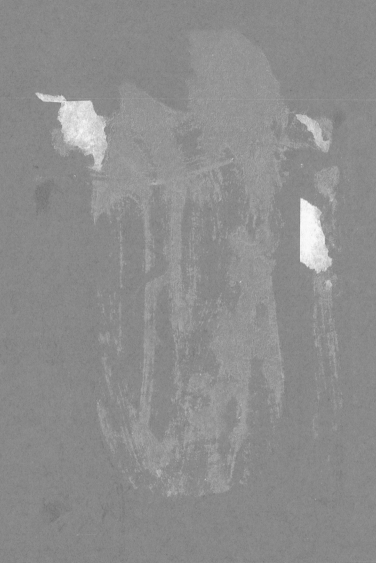

THE WESTMINSTER TANNER-McMURRIN LECTURES
ON THE HISTORY AND PHILOSOPHY OF RELIGION
AT WESTMINSTER COLLEGE

VOLUMES IV AND V

The Westminster Tanner–McMurrin Lectures
on the
History and Philosophy of Religion
at Westminster College

IV
1992

BARBARA C. HARRIS

Suffragan Bishop
The Episcopal Diocese of Massachusetts

WESTMINSTER COLLEGE OF SALT LAKE CITY

THE WESTMINSTER TANNER–McMURRIN
LECTURE SERIES

The Westminster Tanner–McMurrin lectures on the History and Philosophy of Religion were established at Westminster College of Salt Lake City in 1987 as a means of bringing major scholars in the history and philosophy of religion to deliver public lectures and conduct seminars on basic problems in religious thought and practice.

The lecturers are appointed for the national and international recognition of their scholarly achievements without regard to ethnic, national, religious, or ideological considerations.

The lectures are open to the public without charge, and the lecturer conducts seminars in which others who have special interests relating to the subject of the lectures participate by invitation. The lectures are published and made available to libraries and the general public.

The lecture series is administered by the President of Westminster College, who chairs a select committee responsible for lectureship policies and the selection of the lecturers. The Lectureship is funded in perpetuity by an endowment gift from Obert Clark Tanner, Professor Emeritus of Philosophy at the University of Utah, and Grace Adams Tanner. The Lectureship is named in honor of Dr. Sterling M. McMurrin, who is E. E. Ericksen Distinguished Professor Emeritus at the University of Utah and a former United States Commissioner of Education. Dr. McMurrin is a Trustee of Westminster College and a colleague of Dr. Tanner.

THE SELECTION COMMITTEE

CHARLES H. DICK
CHAIR
President, Westminster College of Salt Lake City

CAROLYN TANNER IRISH
*Who has served as an Episcopal Priest,
Dioceses of Michigan, Virginia, and Washington, D.C.*

WILLIAM SMART
*Retired Senior Editor, Deseret News
Salt Lake City, Utah*

STEPHEN BAAR
*Vice President for Academic Affairs and Dean of the Faculty,
Westminster College of Salt Lake City*

MICHAEL POPICH
*Chair, Philosophy and Religion,
Westminster College of Salt Lake City*

SEMINAR PARTICIPANTS
March 27, 1992

THE RIGHT REVEREND GEORGE BATES — *Moderator*
Bishop, The Episcopal Diocese of Utah

THE REVEREND FRANCE A. DAVIS
Pastor, Calvary Baptist Church of Salt Lake City

THE REVEREND JOHN KALOUDIS
Pastor, Holy Trinity Greek Orthodox Church

DR. LAURENCE D. LOEB
Cantor, Congregation Kol Ami
Associate Professor of Anthropology, University of Utah

DR. COLLEEN MCDANNELL
Sterling McMurrin Chair of Religious Studies, University of Utah

THE REVEREND MONSIGNOR M. FRANCIS MANNION
Rector, Cathedral of the Madeleine, Salt Lake Catholic Diocese

THE REVEREND ROBERT J. SCHRANK
Pastor, St. John's Lutheran Church, Missouri Synod

MS. PEGGY FLETCHER STACK
Religion Editor, The Salt Lake Tribune

Beyond Powershift:
Theological Questions in a Changing World

BARBARA C. HARRIS

THE WESTMINSTER TANNER–MCMURRIN LECTURES ON THE
HISTORY AND PHILOSOPHY OF RELIGION

Delivered at

Westminster College of Salt Lake City

March 26, 1992

Barbara Clementine Harris, a native of Philadelphia, graduated from the Charles Price School of Advertising and Journalism. She joined Joseph V. Baker Associates, Inc., a national public relations firm headquartered in Philadelphia, in 1949. She was president of the firm in 1968, when she joined the Sun Company as a community relations consultant. Ms. Harris later was named Manager of Community and Urban Affairs and headed Sun's Public Relations Department from May 1973 until she became a senior staff consultant at Sun's corporate headquarters in January 1977.

Ms. Harris attended Villanova University and studied at the Urban Theology Unit in Sheffield, England. She is a graduate of the Pennsylvania Foundation for Pastoral Counseling. Ordained to the diaconate in September 1979, the Rev. Ms. Harris was ordained a priest in 1980.

Bishop Harris served as Priest-in-charge of St. Augustine of Hippo Church in Norristown, Pennsylvania, from 1980 to 1984. She also served as chaplain to the Philadelphia County prisons and as counsel to industrial corporations for public policy issues and social concerns. In 1984, Bishop Harris was named Executive Director of the Episcopal Church Publishing Company and Publisher of *The Witness* magazine. In 1988 she took on additional duties as Interim Rector of Philadelphia's Church of the Advocate.

In 1984, Barbara Clementine Harris was elected Suffragan (assistant) Bishop of the Diocese of Massachusetts. On February 11, 1989, she was consecrated a bishop — the first woman to be ordained to the episcopate in the Anglican Communion.

Bishop Harris is a member of the Union of Black Episcopalians and is active in a number of professional and community organizations. She represents the national Episcopal Church on the board of the Prisoner Visitation and Support Committee (a ministry in federal and military correctional institutions), is a member of the board of directors of the National Episcopal AIDS Coalition, and is vice-president of Episcopal City Mission, an independent agency within the diocese whose focus is advocacy for and on behalf of the urban poor.

Bishop Harris has received honorary degrees from ten colleges, universities, and theological schools.

It is indeed an honor to have been invited to deliver this year's Westminster Tanner–McMurrin Lecture and to occupy the same podium as my predecessors in this distinguished lecture series. It is a great pleasure and a privilege to be here, and I deeply appreciate the opportunity to share a few thoughts with you on a subject that points us toward the future. That subject is CHANGE.

I would like to look at some of the changes our global society is undergoing with regard to sources of power and some implications of such changes for religion in general and Christian churches in particular. Originally this lecture was titled "Beyond Powershift: Theological Understandings in a Changing World." As I began to develop it, however, several fundamental questions began to emerge for me. It is to these questions I would like to turn your attention and retitle this lecture "Beyond Powershift: Theological Questions *in a Changing World."*

Much of what I want to share is focused against the backdrop of two books I have looked at recently. One is Alvin Toffler's *Powershift: Knowledge, Wealth, and Violence at the Edge of the 21st Century*, and the other is *The Once and Future Church* by the Reverend Loren B. Mead, founder and president of the Alban Institute in Washington, D.C.[1]

Powershift is the third, and probably the last, in a series by Toffler, each of which was intended to lead into the next. The first, *Future Shock*, published in 1971, looks at the process of change and how change affects people and organizations.[2] The second of the trilogy, entitled *The Third Wave*, is a 1984 work

---

[1] Alvin Toffler, *Powershift: Knowledge, Wealth, and Violence at the Edge of the 21st Century* (New York: Bantam Books, 1990); Loren B. Mead, *The Once and Future Church: Reinventing the Congregation for a New Missions Frontier* (Washington, D.C.: The Alban Institute, 1991).

[2] Alvin Toffler, *Future Shock* (New York: Bantam Books, 1971).

that focuses on the direction of change and where changes were taking place at that time.[3] *Powershift* deals with the control of changes still to come — who will shape them and how.

Meanwhile, the burden of Loren Mead's work in *The Once and Future Church* draws our attention, in the author's own words, to "how our vision of the mission of the church came into sharp focus . . . what that vision produced . . . how that clarity came to lose its sharp focus . . . an emerging sense of mission and . . . the kinds of changes that will require ordering our lives within the church." [4] The slim, highly readable volume makes the point that the Church now meets the world in the lives of its laity rather than in foreign mission fields. The brief epigraph cites Mead's belief that denominations once structured to deliver resources to far-off places must now encounter the mission field in the layperson's workplace. Old assumptions no longer work, and church institutions would seem to be breaking down. The new era into which the Church is moving is not yet clear, and the period of transition in which we find ourselves confronts us with challenging dilemmas of what to do in the meantime.[5]

I would note that an acquaintance who formerly taught at the Harvard Business School reports that Toffler is regarded by professionals in his field as a popularizer, but an excellent popularizer, well grounded in what he is talking about and apparently well thought of by academics.

Toffler is notably nonjudgmental in what he says: he first reports facts with a minimum of personal opinion and then offers his conclusions. This is truly noteworthy for anyone writing in this field. Most futurists, in my opinion, and, more importantly, in the opinion of many scholars, play by "hunch" on selected facts. In such a vague field, this is not necessarily bad by any means. I suspect that Toffler would not care to be called a futurist, as he sev-

---

[3] Alvin Toffler, *The Third Wave* (New York: Bantam Books, 1984).
[4] Mead, *The Once and Future Church*, p. 7.
[5] Ibid.

eral times makes note of the imprecision necessarily involved in any speculation about what tomorrow will bring.

Mead is an insightful Episcopal priest who has worked over the last several years with churches and judicatory executives of many denominations. He serves as a consultant to the three bishops of Massachusetts and has assisted us greatly to focus on our present roles as Diocesan, Suffragan and Assistant and on our extended vision for the Church in our own diocese and beyond.

It is well, I believe, to cite some of the basic assumptions that underlie Toffler's work in *Powershift*. Out of some twenty-five, I have chosen six that bear directly on the theological questions I later hope to raise. First and almost embarrassingly obvious:

• Power is inherent in all social systems and in all human relationships. It is not a thing but an aspect of any and all relationships among people. Hence it is inescapable and neutral, intrinsically neither good nor bad.

• Because people have needs and desires, those who can fulfill them hold potential power. Social power is exercised by supplying or withholding the desired or needed items and experiences.

• Because needs and desires are highly varied, the ways of meeting or denying them are also extremely varied. There are, therefore, many different "tools" or "levers" of power. Among them, however, violence, wealth, and knowledge are primary. Most other power resources derive from these.

• Violence, which is chiefly used to punish, is the least versatile source of power. Wealth, which can be used both to reward and punish, and which can be converted into many other resources, is a far more flexible tool of power. Knowledge, however, is the most versatile and basic, since it can help avert challenges that might require the use of violence or wealth, and can often be used to persuade others to perform in desired ways out of perceived self-interest. Knowledge yields the highest quality power.

• Perfect equality implies changelessness, and is not only impossible but undesirable. In a world in which millions starve, the idea of stopping change is not only futile but immoral. The existence of some degree of inequality is not, therefore, inherently immoral; what is immoral is a system that freezes the maldistribution of those resources that give power. It is doubly immoral when that maldistribution is based on race, gender, or other inborn traits.

And last,

> • Knowledge is even more maldistributed than arms and wealth. Hence, a redistribution of knowledge (and especially knowledge about knowledge) is even more important than, and can lead to, a redistribution of the other main power resources.[6]

I would turn now to what I regard as *Powershift*'s summary theme, if you will. Toffler holds that the three traditional sources of power — force (or violence), wealth, and knowledge — are shifting their relationships, and knowledge is taking over as the most effective of the three and is the key to the future. These three sources of power roughly parallel three stages of world history; the agricultural (read muscle), the industrial/smokestack (read money), and the contemporary (read knowledge). We are well into the "third wave," where knowledge increasingly creates power for its holders and its users. Toffler notes: "A 'powershift' does not merely transfer power. It transforms it." [7] The book develops this theory in detail and applies it to developments in business, the economy, politics, and global affairs. The author also notes the place of religion as it affects and is influenced by the contemporary world.[8]

Force and money themselves are becoming increasingly knowledge oriented. Operation Desert Storm is an illustration of the effect of knowledge on warfare, and it is increasingly clear that

---

[6] Toffler, *Powershift*, pp. 467–69.

[7] Ibid., p. 4.

[8] Ibid., pp. 346–47.

the power of business is related to its know-how and not simply to its products and services.

Force, wealth, and knowledge have been variously interpreted in church history and now are embodied in church structure. Loren Mead describes this as the rapidly fading "Christendom Paradigm" that began to emerge in the fourth century, beginning with the conversion of the Emperor Constantine in 313 A.D., and which has held appreciable sway in the life of the Church ever since.[9] The Church, unlike early Christian communities in what Mead refers to as the "Apostolic Age," identified with the Empire. There was no separation between the world and the Church, between sacred and secular. Imperialism and mission were inseparable.

Witness, as Mead points out, that "Bishops were leaders in things we might call secular (raising and deploying armies and playing major political roles, largely as stabilizing forces); kings and princes were leaders in things we might call religious (convening religious convocations and influencing their theological outcomes, just as the Emperor Constantine did at the Council of Nicaea in 325)." [10] And I would add the Crusades; the importation of the Inquisition to the islands of the Caribbean; the religious intolerance and persecutions throughout Europe; and some of the more dubious missionary incursions into Africa, Asia, and North America. Further, the use of force, money, and knowledge for, by, and against the churches is well documented in Edwin Scott Gaustad's *A Religious History of America.*[11]

Mead goes on to observe that the paradigm's importance for us "lies in the fact that most of the generation that now leads our churches grew up with it as a way of thinking about church and society. And all the structures and institutions that make up the churches and the infrastructure of religious life . . . are built on

[9] Mead, *The Once and Future Church*, p. 13.

[10] Ibid., p. 15.

[11] Edwin Scott Gaustad, *A Religious History of America* (Rev. ed., San Francisco: Harper, 1990).

[its] presuppositions" — not so much in the ancient and classical version, but in its nineteenth- and early twentieth-century manifestations.[12] He further says: "Although our Constitution mandates a severe separation of church and state, in fact our nation has lived its own version of the Christendom Paradigm. An informal but fully operational religious establishment has held sway from the beginning — a creature of custom, never of law." [13]

Toffler, meanwhile, makes several compelling observations for the Church throughout *Powershift*. I recommend, as required reading, his material on "Yearnings for a New Dark Age," found in a Coda to an exciting chapter on the proliferation of new communications tools and technologies and tomorrow's Third Wave media, and a section in Chapter 34 entitled "The Resurrection of Religion." [14] Toffler's considerable insights deal with the rise of fundamentalism of all sorts, including that of various ecologists, as a social/psychological rather than a religious phenomenon. Some of these insights include the following:

- Ethnicism and xenophobia are on the rise;
- Earlier religious revival has been followed by fundamentalist extremism in many parts of the world;
- The resurgent religious movements are united in one thing— their hostility to secularism, which is the philosophical base of mass democracy;
- Agents of a new "Dark Age" represent movements that combine totalitarianism with universalism;
- The fundamentalist basically wants to return to the earlier (read: agricultural) world, in which force or violence is the source of all power. The need for personal control is clear in such a wish; the intention is not so much to avoid any change as it is to control all change in ways acceptable and desirable to the fundamentalist; and

[12] Mead, *The Once and Future Church*, p. 18.
[13] Ibid., p. 20.
[14] Toffler, *Powershift*, pp. 364–79, 450–52.

• In the Powershift era ahead, the primary ideological struggle will be between twenty-first-century democracy and eleventh-century darkness.

My own reading of the situation leads me to observe that there would seem to be a fundamentalism of the heart that is attracted by any certainty, and it may yet be the death of us all. There are those who will only call themselves Christian to selected people because they will not be associated with many others who call themselves Christians and who use their faith only to push others around, if not bash them to death. Perhaps a most basic question is: What kind of a god do fundamentalists really believe in? There is serious doubt that their god has any affinity with the God of the old-line churches, but few dare say this. It is said that Archbishop Temple once remarked that one of our major responsibilities as Christians is to be jealous for the integrity of God. I am not sure we do this with any intention or consistency, and that may just be the greatest sin of which we are guilty.

In a recent paper, one of our diocesan staff members suggests, and I would agree, that perhaps the primary reason for division within the Church has to do with the cultural captivity of the Gospel, in which individuals and groups seek to use the Church to legitimate their own identity, power, and status rather than seeking to transform their identity, power, and status to the demands of the Gospel. Seen in this light, the continued racial segregation in the Church in this country is one clear and vivid example of this cultural captivity. When understood for what it is, segregation lies at the root of so much of the debate within the Episcopal Church and other denominations over issues of inclusivity, traditional values, and fundamentalism. The latter are but surface issues which, at face value, constitute sources of discord, but which, in fact, mask deeper cultural proclivities.

Rather than fighting among ourselves, our staff member continues, over what should be the Christian world view or, more precisely, over which is preeminent among the various world views which exist within Christianity, we would be better served to acknowledge that, like Paul speaking on the plaza to the unknown God, we confront a world that no longer understands or respects any version of the Christian world view. The failure to recognize this reality as our present context leads to the deeper frustration and sense of alienation that biblical fundamentalists and self-styled traditionalists in my own denomination feel, as a result of the world's rejection of their myopic and self-serving Gospel. This is at the heart of the tension within the Episcopal Church and others between the so-called traditionalists and those who are seeking to adapt the Church and its message to the changing societal scene.

Some churches, particularly those more fundamentalist in nature, still are trying to use force to compel acquiescence with "truth." The decreasing revenues of virtually all churches indicate our present very real difficulties, but perhaps for other reasons than those generally attributed. Every dollar lost is power lost, and that lost power is not being replaced by increases in knowledge.

The use of church wealth in a changing society is an area that demands not only consideration but thoughtful examination as well. In the Powershift era, churches need to examine effective utilization of this source of power which, for most mainline denominations, is diminishing. This would suggest some honest appraisal of our history and our present practice in light of Loren Mead's "Christendom Paradigm."

In truth, churches have been focused more on survival and charity than on justice, which is compassion or love distributed. A rough distinction would suggest that charity is the giving from one's surplus to the individual or cause of one's choice. It is usually painless and selective. Justice is sacrificial giving, or the process by which greater equity is established between individuals and groups. It rarely is painless and, in most instances, involves struggle for systemic change.

Some easily recognizable additional characteristics are: charity usually is passive, supports the status quo, is low risk, is "band-aid" in nature, can create enmity, and is nonpolitical, pastoral, and individual. Justice, on the other hand, usually is active, brings about change, and is non-selective, high-risk, systemic, long-term, political, prophetic, and collective.

The road from charity to justice represents a transformation of wealth to knowledge as a source of power. That road, however, is marked by more questions than directional signs. Some of those questions include: (1) Can one-dimensional social service ministries, which have been our history and mark much of our present practice, be maintained in the face of increasingly overwhelming need? (2) At what point must charity cease and demands for systemic change commence? (3) Can systemic change activity exist in isolation from the persons and situations for whom change is desired? (4) What are the limits of private-sector initiatives, and how do these translate into Church structures with their various levels of focus for ministry? and, (5) What is the ecumenical option for such a time?

Can one-dimensional social service ministries be maintained in the face of increasingly overwhelming need? A simple answer, of course, is "no." The point I would like to make is that the Church has been so easily motivated by guilt to get involved in certain ministries that it has been blinded to recognizing when the point of diminishing return has been reached. An important element in any analysis, therefore, needs to be the discipline of reflection which constantly challenges negative motives, helps maintain objectivity, and enables honest evaluation of the utility of any ministry or program. The key ingredient is spiritual grounding in the love ethic which, by definition, recognizes the finite nature of human endurance. As we move into an even more difficult period of economic decline, government cutbacks, and increased competition for scarce resources, churches must develop a process of spiritual toughness that will enable them to make the "triage" decisions necessary.

Serious thought must be given to an understanding of steward-
ship on the income side and fiduciary responsibility on the expense
side. That is to say, the rainy day against which churches have
husbanded their resources is at hand, and concern for the welfare
of our posterity must focus on salvaging our current society so that
there will be a posterity.

Nowhere is this more clearly seen than in the situation of
HIV/AIDS where, in the absence of a cure, radical changes in our
lifestyles and values are required if humankind is to exist. Without playing out this analogy to its extreme, one can easily see how
the virtues of prudence and conservation take on new meaning
with regard to current assets. Similarly, the environmental crisis
spurs us to a profound reexamination of our values, lifestyle
choices, and use of natural resources. The real question we must
face is how thorough an analysis are we prepared to make of our
internal and external contradictions in order to advocate the necessary changes in social policy which, if properly construed, will
eventuate in a just, equitable, sustainable, and accessible society?
In other words, the bigger the problem, the larger the solution,
and the more profound the cost. Clarity on this macro level is a
prerequisite for informed action on specific micro issues.

Can systemic change activity exist in isolation from the persons
and situations for whom change is desired? Where the previous
question calls us to a profound rearticulation of our spiritual
values, which in turn will inform our economic, political, and
social arrangements, they will only have meaning to the degree
that they positively impact the lives of the hungry, the homeless,
the sick, and the dying. Ivory-towered analysis without a firm
grounding in the reality of human suffering is an affront to the
people, and apocalyptic prognostications are more apt to engender
a sense of powerlessness and paralysis than action that leads to
redemption. A simple way to put this is to say that we do not need
a liberation theology that is politically correct but unworkable.
We need a liberation methodology which overcomes polarization,

fosters true equality, and actually changes the lives and conditions of people.

What is the ecumenical option at this time? While all religious institutions are undergoing the same stress, is this not a time to come to some common understandings about priorities and responses? The old adage that two heads are better than one takes on new meaning in the crisis of change, and since we are all in the same boat, there is no excuse for not testing the limits of cooperation that new circumstances present. Whole sectors of human services are collapsing, including housing, education, health, and welfare. Individual church bodies have at least three options. One is to walk away from the situation and hope the storm will pass. A second is to expend all their resources in one grand explosion of concern and then walk away. Or they can overcome issues of turf, polity, and ownership and become creative in reducing overhead so that maximum resources can be channeled into commonly agreed-upon priorities over time. Although we may never live to see the full flowering of this vision, it at least needs to be lifted up as a reasonable option for all churches to consider.

Mainline denominations might be surprised to discover that they have much to learn from other churches about how to survive with meager resources, and the latter might also have some creative suggestions about putting mainline churches' relative abundance to more practical use. In either case, the era ahead will not be a time to stand on historical differences born out of a distant cultural past but rather a time to examine whether new occasions can indeed teach new duties as time makes ancient good uncouth!

In this light, how must each of the three major sources of power be changed if traditional churches are to be useful to the larger society or even to survive in the era ahead? At the same time it is appropriate to question whether the churches should be analyzed in power terms at all. Both we and the non-church world do this, and that fact ignores issues of the appropriateness and the moral validity of such analyses.

In the area of knowledge we must ask: What do churches and Christians KNOW? Our knowledge is vague, at the least. Perhaps this is why rigid groups that do have "certain" knowledge are growing while others are not. How can we teach and share our knowledge? Can traditional ecclesiastical "power" be maintained, and is it desirable to do so, even if we could? There is no unanimity in oldline churches about what the church is for, much less what the content of the gospel is. Can we possibly offer anything to the world that it cannot more efficiently get elsewhere, and, if so, what is that "anything"?

A primary problem in a knowledge-is-power world is to find out what our work in the world as Christians is. We must be clear and articulate about what we want to do and how power can help accomplish it. A second problem which is related to the first, and is nearly as significant, concerns the place and interaction of clergy and lay persons within churches and their institutions.

Discussions of power appear to be even more offensive to most churchpeople than discussions of issues of both death and sexuality, despite the fact that on the parochial, judicatory, and national levels everyone plays power games. If power is the ability to act and knowledge is a source of power, it is equally available to all Christians, and the traditional roles of clergy and lay persons will change. We can either react to such change or control it by initiating it. Our first job is to determine what our work is, and the second is to decide how power-as-knowledge can be shared by ALL baptized persons.

There is already in place a new production paradigm, which Toffler calls "the super-symbolic economy." [15] Productivity as well as power is based on knowledge rather than labor and material; connectivity rather than disconnectedness; integration rather than disintegration; real-time simultaneity rather than sequential stages.

What does this mean in terms of ourselves and the education, not only of our own children, but of children around the world?

[15] Ibid., Part Two: "Life in the Super-Symbolic Economy," pp. 21–88.

What it implies, as does so much else these days, is that the gulf between the haves and the have-nots is deepening, fostered deliberately, in my opinion, by the former. Any child, for example, who does not become computer literate is well on his or her way to being permanently unemployed and economically disenfranchised.

Toffler also presents incontrovertible evidence that nations, the United States being a prime example, are becoming increasingly ungovernable. What he says about nations is also true of most large institutions. The churches, for example, nearly all of which are under the control of or in the power of an elite of one sort or another — generally white and male — are operating directly counter to the worldwide trend toward grass-roots organizations centered on a myriad of political, social, and cultural LOCAL causes. Put in ecclesiastical terms, we might ask, for example, how much longer will a congregation give its judicatory and national church structures anything when the hungry are at its own church doors and cannot, in the vast majority of cases, be helped by regional or national programs?

The sheer size of institutions contributes to their unworkability, as do levels of middle management that no longer are necessary to their well being. As we know, the more people involved in the administration of an institution, the more important — and the more difficult — communication among them is. Essential to the exchange of information that creates power in the contemporary world is instant local and worldwide communication. Churches, except for a group of self-serving televangelists and the Roman Catholics, the Mormons, and the Christian Scientists, seldom have used modern electronic communications at all, much less well. They rely on bulletins, newsletters, and other printed materials to the exclusion of the many contemporary means of communication.

If my suspicion is correct, one reason we have not used electronic media is not because of a lack of money, rather a lack of message.

Bureaucracy simply does not work in a world whose primary source of power is knowledge, because it is built on three assumptions that no longer are valid: (1) that knowledge can be cubby-holed, as opposed to integrated; (2) that information must travel through channels in a vertical hierarchy; and (3) that large problems (such as AIDS) can be handled by only one agency. The traditional levels of middle management are going by the board very quickly because knowledge can travel both laterally and "to the top" much more quickly and efficiently than through the vertical hierarchy that characterizes bureaucracy. Tomorrow's world is one in which everybody can and will be a conveyor of knowledge as well as its recipient. This, of course, opens doors for all sorts of demagogues, including religious ones.

One hesitates even to reflect on what all this means for churches and their institutions. The necessity for judicatorial assistant executives, such as suffragan bishops, may disappear altogether, assuming it has not already. Similarly, traditional church structures are well on their way to becoming obsolete, if they have not already.

Loren Mead suggests that our task is no less than the reinvention of the church.[16] No simple task, he sees this as the work of several generations. Over time they must struggle with some painful polarities as well as structural issues. Among the former are concepts such as "Parish versus Congregation"; "Servanthood versus Conversion"; and the Church's image of itself as "Exclusive or Inclusive."[17] "It is within the tension of these polarities," Mead maintains, "that the church will be called on to address the formation of its laity, the new roles [or "reformation"] of the clergy, the function of oversight, and the locus of theology."[18] While citing several impediments to such radical and virtual total restructure, Mead nonetheless proposes a church turned upside down to exercise ministry on a changed mission frontier.

But let us return to Toffler for just a moment. Because knowledge is now the power base, mega-firms are appearing. According

16 Mead, *The Once and Future Church*, p. 43.

17 Ibid., Chapter IV, "The Reinvention of the Church," pp. 43–68.

18 Ibid., p. 48.

to Toffler, the term "multinational" is no longer applicable. "Mega-firms are essentially nonnational." [19] What this means is, frighteningly enough, that their primary loyalty is to the firm or its field and not even to the nation in which they began or the wider world in which they operate. Munitions firms, for example, will sell to anyone, and a government like our own enables them to do so by playing their games.

Are, can, or should churches be inclusive in this "mega" sense? Churches have said that our highest loyalty is to God, no matter what our nation may be. There is little evidence that we really believe this, and it would probably lead us to a political mega-ism similar to that of Roman Catholicism. I would note, as well, that ecumenicity, as it has been preached and practiced in a very limited way, has never been a realistic goal in this mega-sense. Where ecumenicity still is meaningful is in local associations of congregations coalesced to feed the hungry or shelter the homeless. In the light of what Toffler is saying, the larger ecumenical movement is dead unless churches are willing, as I pointed out in my earlier observations, to think in terms of knowledge-based interactivity, rather than theological or doctrinal "sharing."

If we are to give any serious consideration to the premises of these two authors, and I think we should, I would suggest that we raise among ourselves some fundamental questions. How can we bring the church and its institutions into the contemporary world? How can we re-form these organizations to use their good intentions for the wider world's benefit as well as that of Christians? What is the place of clergy, if any, in a newly re-formed church? Would we be better off to close down our present operations and start again, as impossible as that might seem?

What can we do about our own counterproductive educational habits, much less assist in non-church education as it needs to be practiced in the wider world? What is it that we, as Christians, have to teach people and want to teach them? Or, perhaps more

[19] Toffler, *Powershift*, p. 454.

honestly, what do we have to learn ourselves, and how do we go about sharing it?

Moreover, will we address the real questions of our disunity as faithful people? Can Christians find anything at all to focus on as a uniting force? Christ, we proclaim, is the answer to every question, but it is the questions to which he is expected to be the answer that hold in bold relief our disunity, our fragmentation, and our inertia.

As I noted at the outset, I have in fact raised more questions than provided answers or understandings. Given the radical changes that are taking place about us, this is as it should be. However, as a bishop of the church and as a baptized Christian, there are some concluding comments I feel compelled to make to balance the skeptical tone of this lecture.

As people of faith, we believe that the greatest source of power is God's love for us as revealed in the ministry, death, and resurrection of Jesus Christ. It was Frederick Douglass, the great abolitionist of the nineteenth century, who observed in his famous oration on change that those who wish change to be easy or peaceful are like those who wish rain without lightning and thunder, the beauty of the ocean without the tumult of its mighty roar, or salvation without judgment. He concluded that famous speech with the observation, "You don't get everything that you pay for in this world, but you must pay for everything that you get." Certainly no one can deny the existential validity of this observation. Yet, as Christians, we also know that the one thing we have not paid for and which is the exception to this rule is God's gift of grace to us, and the power that can come from living in the Gospel of Christ Jesus our Lord.

While the observations of Toffler, Mead, and other futurists may shock some of us, alarm others, and even paralyze yet others, I have lived long enough and seen too much to believe that the Church, when it is true to itself and to its God, is incapable of meeting the challenge of this new age. The test for us is in our capacity to embrace change as growth, which is necessary for the survival of all living organisms, and to trust in God's grace to direct our thoughts and actions into the right paths of change for the building up of his kingdom. To do less is to avoid the call to follow Christ wherever he may lead us, believing that all things ultimately work together for good for those who love God.

The Westminster Tanner–McMurrin Lectures on the History and Philosophy of Religion at Westminster College

V
1993

RALPH McINERNY

Michael P. Grace Professor of Medieval Studies
University of Notre Dame

WESTMINSTER COLLEGE OF SALT LAKE CITY

THE SELECTION COMMITTEE

CHARLES H. DICK
CHAIR

President, Westminster College of Salt Lake City

STEPHEN R. BAAR

Vice President for Academic Affairs and Dean of the Faculty, Westminster College of Salt Lake City

CAROLYN TANNER IRISH

Who has served as an Episcopal Priest, Dioceses of Michigan, Virginia, and Washington, D.C.

MICHAEL A. POPICH

Chair, Philosophy and Religion, Westminster College of Salt Lake City

CLAUDINE CORBETT WILCOX

Executive Assistant to the President, Westminster College of Salt Lake City

SEMINAR PARTICIPANTS
February 26, 1993

THE REVEREND MONSIGNOR M. FRANCIS MANNION —
Moderator

Rector, Cathedral of the Madeleine, Salt Lake Catholic Diocese

DR. PETER C. APPLEBY

*Associate Professor and Chair, Department of Philosophy,
University of Utah*

ELDER J. RICHARD CLARKE

*Member of the Presidency of the Quorum of the Seventy,
Church of Jesus Christ of Latter-day Saints*

THE REVEREND JOHN KALOUDIS

Pastor, Holy Trinity Greek Orthodox Church

THE REVEREND CARYL A. MARSH

Rector, St. Paul's Episcopal Church

DR. JENNINGS G. OLSON

Professor Emeritus of Philosophy, Weber State University

DR. MICHAEL A. POPICH

Associate Professor of Philosophy, Westminster College of Salt Lake City

THE REVEREND ROBERT J. SCHRANK

Pastor, St. John's Lutheran Church, Missouri Synod

RABBI FREDERICK L. WENGER

Congregation Kol Ami

The God of Philosophers

RALPH McINERNY

THE WESTMINSTER TANNER–MCMURRIN LECTURES ON THE
HISTORY AND PHILOSOPHY OF RELIGION

Delivered at

Westminster College of Salt Lake City

February 25, 1993

RALPH MATTHEW McINERNY, an Irish Catholic Midwesterner, was born in Minneapolis. He grew up in the Twin Cities, served a year with the U.S. Marine Corps, and entered the diocesan seminary in St. Paul, Minnesota. By 1951, when he received his bachelor's degree at St. Paul Seminary, Professor McInerny had decided on an academic career in lieu of the priesthood. He earned a master's degree in philosophy and classics at the University of Minnesota and went on to take his Ph.D. (*summa cum laude*) at Laval University in Quebec.

On January 3, 1953, he married Constance Kunert (the "Connie" to whom many of his books are dedicated), and they have a family of six children and ten grandchildren.

After a one-year teaching stint at Creighton University, Professor McInerny and his wife settled in South Bend, Indiana, in 1955, where he took on an instructorship in philosophy at the University of Notre Dame. He advanced steadily through the academic ranks until he was made Professor of Philosophy in 1969. Since 1978, he has been the Michael P. Grace Professor of Medieval Studies at Notre Dame, Director of the Jacques Maritain Center, and, until 1985, Director of the Medieval Institute.

The recipient of two honorary Doctor of Letters degrees, Professor McInerny has been a guest lecturer at more than fifty colleges and universities. In 1982 he co-founded *Crisis* with Michael Novak, a journal of lay Catholic opinion which attempts to reassert the "broad sane center of Catholic thought." Professor McInerny was for eleven years the editor of the philosophic journal *The New Scholasticism*. The most recent of his many scholarly works are *A First Glance at St. Thomas Aquinas: Handbook for Peeping Thomists* (1990), *Aquinas on Human Action* (1992), and *Aquinas Against the Averroists* (1993). He is a prolific writer of novels as well, and his Father Dowling mysteries enjoy international popularity.

At half past ten on the evening of November 23, 1654, Blaise Pascal had a religious experience which changed his life. In what came to be called the Memorial, he jotted down what had happened to him. It is from the Memorial that I take the title for this lecture.

"Fire," Pascal wrote, and then, "God of Abraham, God of Isaac, God of Jacob, *not* the God of the philosophers . . ."

Kierkegaard once said of Holy Scripture that it is like a mirror — if a monkey looks in, no apostle looks out. So it is, all proportions guarded, with such a document as Pascal's Memorial. The average worldly person — *l'homme moyen sensuel* — reads it and reads words. 'Certainty.' 'Feeling.' 'Joy.' 'Peace.' "*Grandeur de l'âme humaine.*" But one would have to be hardened indeed not to sense something of the tremendous experience memorialized. Pascal had an experience of God, and he contrasts it with what philosophers have had to say about the supreme being. That is my subject.

I propose to deal with it by laying before you some thoughts of Sören Kierkegaard, the great nineteenth-century Danish Lutheran, and following that up with some thoughts derived from St. Thomas Aquinas.[1]

1. SOME KIERKEGAARDIAN REMINDERS

Kierkegaard (1813–1855) took on the task of reintroducing Christianity to Christendom. He felt that the faith had become so domesticated that Christians ran the danger of thinking they were Christians in much the same way they were Danes, male or female, blonds or brunettes — it was an accident of birth, a geographical

---

[1] I am in my modest way a Thomist, that is, one whose thought has been profoundly shaped by decades of study of the Angelic Doctor. But at the outset of my graduate studies, at the University of Minnesota, I was introduced to Kierkegaard by Professor Paul Holmer. I cannot imagine thinking about the topic of this paper without having recourse to Kierkegaard.

[7]

or national designation, something that *happened* to you more or less unbidden. Christian faith had, in short, become naturalized, domesticated and, Kierkegaard feared, trivialized.

Of course, simply to have said this would have been to produce more of the kind of discourse that had become domesticated. One of the things believers become used to is the reminder that there is a distance between their profession and their practice. What has been lost is the wonder of salvation, the sense of sin, the need for redemption, the awe and gratitude at God's having become man. And of course this too is part and parcel of what believers are used to hearing. In order to cope with this situation, Kierkegaard devised a system of what he called *indirect communication*, which he hoped would enable him to overcome the obstacles to making the point he wished to make. That point, put most simply, was that Christians are confused as to what Christianity is. Philosophers, he felt, have their own peculiar way of misunderstanding Christianity. That is why he created a special pseudonym, Johannes Climacus, to deal with the philosophical misunderstanding of Christianity.

Actually, Johannes Climacus shows up first in the Kierkegaardian literature as the titular hero of an unfinished novel, the subtitle of which is *De omnibus dubitandum est*. The Johannes of the story was a university student of philosophy who is told by his professors that, as a first step toward becoming a philosopher, he must cast a jaundiced eye on everything he hitherto thought he knew. Only by passing through the cleansing bath of methodic doubt can claims to know achieve reliability. In short, *de omnibus dubitandum est*. Kierkegaard imagined Johannes seeking to follow this advice and thereby landing in all kinds of outlandish situations, much to the surprise, horror, and dismay of his professors. The presumed point of the story is that the advice given cannot really be followed. When Johannes Climacus became one of Kierkegaard's platoon of pseudonyms — pseudonyms are an essential part of indirect communication — his writings were meant to describe a movement "Away from philosophy"! Away from philosophy taken as a misunderstanding of the nature of Christianity.

Two books are attributed to the pseudonym Johannes Climacus, the *Philosophical Fragments* and *Concluding Unscientific Postscript to the Philosophical Fragments*. I doubt that there are many more important books to have come out of the nineteenth century, and I cannot imagine anyone interested in the philosophy of religion failing to find them endlessly provocative.

The Socratic Teacher

The *Fragments* begins by reminding us of certain aspects of the situation in which one human person learns from another. Climacus appropriately selects the historical figure Socrates who, you remember, disclaimed being anything more than a midwife in the process in which his interlocutor came to know something he did not previously know. In making use of Socrates, Climacus may seem to be directing our attention to the *peculiarities* of the Socratic method, as if the maieutic character of teaching were true only of the dialectical strategies of Socrates. But this is far from being the case. Socrates is meant to stand for any account of coming to know, not just one of the many accounts we come upon in the history of philosophy.

Climacus is able to do this by concentrating on the generic aspects of Socrates's teaching. Socrates assumes that his hearer has the capacity to understand — he does not confer this on him. All things being equal, a person can activate this capacity. Sometimes, unaided by others, we come to know things we previously did not know. Teaching, we might say, is a more economical way of passing from *possibly* knowing to *actually* knowing something or other. The teacher facilitates this passage. But, again, he assumes in his hearer, and does not confer upon him, the capacity to know. If the hearer comes to know, this is something he does. The teacher is thus only an occasion of his coming to know, since, when he knows, he is no longer dependent upon the teacher.

For example, there was once a time in my scarcely remembered childhood when I did not know that the sum of the internal angles of a plane triangle is equal to 180 degrees. It is difficult to imagine let alone recall what life was like in the darkness in which I then dwelt, but in any case, I have long since emerged from it. This emergence took place when I was taught geometry. Now, if you asked me who taught me this particular truth about triangles, I would have to think. If you asked me when precisely I came to know it, I could not answer. That all-but-anonymous teacher was the occasion, but he drops out of the picture: he is not included in what I know. No more does the time at which I acquired this truth matter. Even if I kept a diary, I would not expect to find an entry that would record the event. "Today, for the first time, I saw that the sum of the internal angles . . . etc." And even if I had — strange child — made such an entry, it is doubtful to the extreme that I would have employed the heightened language of Pascal's Memorial.

Is this just an accident of memory? Let us say that whenever I think of plane triangles, fond thoughts of Miss Mansfield also occur, and I *do* recall that April afternoon when rain ran down the panes of the schoolroom windows like tears, when there was the fierce smell of lilac in the air, when a hush fell over us as Miss Mansfield turned toward us from the blackboard so that the full impact of the demonstrations she had written there could be felt. *Quod erat demonstrandum!* It hit me like a ton of bricks. I will never forget that moment. Does this destroy Kierkegaard's point?

His point is not that we should not cherish such memories and entertain such fond thoughts of our mentors of yore. Rather his point is that *what* I then came to know does not include any dependence on Miss Mansfield. In fact my memory makes Climacus's point. Miss Mansfield was the occasion of my learning something, and I am grateful to her. But it could have been a substitute. I might have missed the point and been helped by my father to see it. Others have hit upon the truth in question either alone or with

the aid of someone else. In that sense it is quite accidental that
Miss Mansfield played this role for me.

It is clear, then, that Socrates functions in the *Philosophical
Fragments* for any teacher, for every human being who is the
occasion for another human being's coming to know what he did
not hitherto know. Climacus makes the peculiarly Socratic point
that all learning is remembering stand for the fact that every
human being possesses the capacity to know. There is of course a
Socratic theory of teaching that is merely one among several
theories, but it is no part of Socrates's role in the *Fragments* to
argue for his theory *insofar as it differs from other theories*. The
Socratic teacher, in short, is any human teacher.

And now Climacus puts a crucial question. Is there a non-
Socratic teacher? Is there any teacher whose activity does not
exemplify what these reflections on Socrates have reminded us of?
An obvious way to seek the answer to the question is simply to
negate the features of teacher and learner as usually understood
and ask if the resultant negative description applies to anyone.

A Non-Socratic Teacher

The non-Socratic teacher, accordingly, would be one who did
not presume that the learner had the capacity to receive the truth
he offers. To sharpen this difference, we might add that this is not
simply a lack in the learner, but is rather something antagonistic
in him. Thus, if the learner learns from the non-Socratic teacher,
his original indisposition or hostility will have to be dealt with,
and the teacher will have to give him the capacity to receive the truth
and not simply the truth. Such a learner's relation to the teacher
could not recede into the past; it continues. Indeed, the teacher
becomes essential to the truth attained: in a sense the teacher *is* that
truth. Furthermore, the time at which the capacity and the truth
are conferred does not vanish into forgetfulness but is crucial.

Climacus, indefatigable fellow, goes on. We might call the
indisposition on the part of the learner in this non-Socratic situa-

tion Sin; and since the non-Socratic teacher brings about a new man, freeing him from Sin, in order to teach him truth, we might call him Savior, Redeemer. The time at which this occurs might be called the Fullness of Time. And so on.

Kierkegaard's reader has long since begun to guess that Climacus is not describing a merely hypothetical situation. He is reminding the Christian that it would be a mistake to think of Christ on the model of Socrates.

The point of the *Philosophical Fragments*, directly stated, is that it is a mistake to confuse Christ with a merely human teacher. Nonetheless philosophers have a tendency to treat Christian revelation as if it were a body of truths to be appraised in the same way other truth-claims are. Perhaps these truths too should be regarded with methodic doubt, considered with a cold eye to see if they can survive our skepticism. It may of course be that simple folk regard Christianity as made up of impenetrable mysteries, but sophisticated people like university professors will reflect on Christianity as they do other things.

Put into the direct mode, we can say that the philosophical confusion as to the nature of Christianity is to regard it as a set of truths to be appraised in the usual way. Christ then becomes just another teacher, the addressee of Revelation is taken to be in a condition to assess and accept Christian truth in the same way as he learns geometry or physics. The indirect way in which Kierkegaard's pseudonym introduces the non-Socratic teacher makes it clear that, although Christ is never mentioned, the failure to see that Christ is a non-Socratic teacher is in effect to reject Christianity, not to assimilate it.

Kierkegaard's actual historical target was Hegel, and, as with Socrates, we can ask whether what he has to say applies only to Hegel. Later on I will mention the importance of Hegel's emphasis on history for Climacus's description of Christianity. For now I wish to make the point that Hegel stands for any believer who sees faith as a condition to be overcome in this life, not by ceasing to accept Christianity as true, but by claiming to have established its truth by sophisticated means unavailable to the unwashed. As over against this, Climacus says that the only difference between the simple and the wise with respect to Christianity is that the simple do not understand it, and the wise understand that they do not understand it.

What Kierkegaard, through Climacus, is underscoring is the difference between *knowledge and faith*. Indeed, he describes faith as the withholding of a repellent reaction to what seems to reason to be an absurdity. To believe in Jesus is to believe in the union of the divine and human, of the eternal and temporal. But such conjunctions or identifications are paradoxical. To accept the revelation that God has become man is not done on the basis of understanding it, of comprehending it, of seeing that it makes perfect sense and fits in well with all the other things one knows. *Au contraire*. The Incarnation, like the Trinity and most of the other articulations to be found in the Nicene Creed, is a *mystery*. One cannot in this life *understand* the mysteries of faith.

2. THOMAS AQUINAS

I have phrased the point Kierkegaard is making through Johannes Climacus in such a way that his agreement with Thomas Aquinas is evident. Like Kierkegaard, Thomas distinguishes between faith — the theological virtue, the gift thanks to which we adhere to revealed truth — and knowledge — the intellectual virtue whereby we grasp truths about things which are either self-evident or derivable from non-gainsayable truths.[2]

To believe something to be true is often done on the basis of our confidence in some authority. Yorick, a student with a propeller on his cap and a fixed gaze, assures me that a new program

[2] It is not, of course, that we do not speak of what we believe in terms of knowledge ("I know that my redeemer liveth") or of knowledge in terms of belief. What Thomas is proposing is a special use of 'believe' which distinguishes it sharply from a special use of 'know.' The accounts I have given in the text indicate how the distinction is expressed.

will enable me to use my computer in a significantly more effective way. I take his word because such statements of his in the past have proved to be trustworthy. If someone asks me why I speak with such confidence about the merits of Baffle (pat. pend.), I invoke my student Yorick. My interlocutor may then say, "Aha. So you *believe* this to be true; you don't *know* it." Of course he is right, and his triumphalist remark clarifies the distinction we are after.

Mysteries of the Faith

So it is with the mysteries of Christianity. If we give our assent to them as true, we do so because we accept the authority of God who reveals them. There are, needless to say, important differences between trusting Yorick and trusting Yahweh. Taunted by my colleagues, I may purchase a copy of Baffle (pat. pend.), install it in my computer, and emerge from my study a few hours later prepared to assert that I *know* that Baffle has the qualities I earlier asserted of it on the authority of Yorick. Now I speak *in propria persona*, out of my experience. I know, I no longer believe. Divine faith, in this life, does not permit its replacement by knowledge. We would find it odd to hear someone say that, while he used to believe there is a trinity of persons in the Godhead, now he knows this to be true; or that he used to believe that Jesus is human and divine, but now he knows this.[3] (There is more to be said on this, of course, but let us postpone consideration of such matters.)

If it is the case, as I think it is, that Kierkegaard and Thomas are in agreement on the mysteries of faith, it is also the case that there are significant disagreements between the two on the relation between the philosopher and the faith. The differences can be turned around the Pascalian phrase that provides our title: how do the two men stand on the God of the Philosophers?

---

[3] "Odd" if the transition is meant to be the same as that made with respect to Baffle (pat. pend.).

Johannes Climacus not only contests the effort to reduce the mysteries of faith to knowledge-claims of the usual sort; he also rejects the philosophical effort to prove the existence of God. In this Kierkegaard reflects the mentality of the Reformers. No need to recall what Luther had to say about reason, let alone Aristotle. Prior to the Reform, nothing was more common than to find Christian theologians who held *both* that what God has revealed about Himself may be believed but cannot be known in this life, *and* that it is possible to formulate a sound proof for the existence of God. Thomas Aquinas may fittingly stand for all such theologians.

Thomas Aquinas holds that there are two kinds of truth about God. The first kind is all those truths about God which can be established on the basis of what we know about the world: these are the truths we find established even by the pagan philosophers, most especially Aristotle. That God exists, that there is only one God, that the world depends upon God both in order to be and to be what it is, that God is a knowing cause — these and other truths about God can be established by way of arguments which rely only on principles available to all, believer and non-believer alike. The second kind of truth about God is those we have called Mysteries — their truth cannot be established by argument on the basis of what everyone knows. There is, then, for Thomas, a God of the Philosopher.

Indeed, we find among the writings of Thomas philosophical as well as theological works. Philosophical works are characterized by arguments which ultimately rely on truths that everybody already knows. This is as true of the speculative order as it is of the practical order; that is, there are such theoretical first principles as the principle of contradiction, nongainsayable truths which are the conditions of human discourse because they express the way things are. *And* there are such undeniable principles of action as those which make up Natural Law (and are expressed in the Decalogue). Believers and non-believers communicate thanks to these shared, common principles of discourse.

Thomas notices that pagan philosophers, notably Aristotle —
he knew Plato only indirectly — fashioned arguments which pro-
fess to show that there is a first cause of the world and its con-
stituents — God — and descriptions of what he is like. As philosophical, such talk about God, or theology, relies on truths accessible to everyone. Thus, Aristotle's proofs take off from truths
about the world — the fact of motion, that whatever is moved is
moved by another, but there is not an infinite series of moved
movers. The proof succeeds or fails insofar as it is cogently based
on such easily accessible truths. Thomas thinks Aristotle's proof
works and that he arrived at truths about God.

An obvious objection to this will occur to you. The list of
truths about God philosophers are said to have shown — that
there is a God, that there cannot be more than one God, etc. —
are part of what God has revealed about Himself. Indeed, his
existence might be said to be the primary, in the sense of the most
basic, thing He reveals to us. But if the truths God has revealed to
us are the object of faith, not knowledge, Thomas seems deprived
of any basis for saying they can be known, even by philosophers.

Preambles and Mysteries

To this Thomas would reply that when he made the distinction
between the two kinds of truth about God, he meant to distinguish
among *revealed* truths. If philosophers can prove the existence of
God, and if the existence of God is revealed, then not everything
that has been revealed *must necessarily* be accepted on the basis of
faith. It looks as if God has revealed things about himself that we
are capable of coming to know, as well as many more things that
we would be unaware of apart from revelation. Thomas calls such
truths *praeambula fidei*, Preambles of Faith, as opposed to Mysteries of Faith.

Climacus argues that attempts to prove the existence of God
must fail because we cannot prove the existence of *anything*. We
can discuss what properties an existent thing does or does not

have, but its existence is not among the things we can prove. That
is clearly wrong; it makes perfectly good sense to say that the existence of a new galaxy has been proved. But even if one rejected
the general stricture against proofs of existence, he might well
hold that the existence of *God* cannot be proved. As a matter of
fact, if you should poll a classroom of undergraduates at my university on the question, "Can the existence of God be proved?"
the results would be overwhelmingly negative. The reasons for
this are far more Pascalian than anything else — but it is to that I
have already promised to return.

Before doing that, however, I want to draw attention to the
importance for Thomas of the recognition of naturally knowable
truths about God, the *praeambula fidei*, for the question of the
reasonableness of religious faith.

Johannes Climacus, if not Kierkegaard himself, leaves us with
the impression that faith is a kind of defiant acceptance of the
absurd; his is almost a *Credo quia absurdum* position. Climacus
seems to revel in the thought that Christianity is not simply different from reason, distinct from it, but is also in conflict with it.
It is almost as if to believe were to accept as true what one knows
to be false. That is the most exaggerated form of the position and
cannot be ascribed to Kierkegaard himself nor, save by way of
intimation, to his pseudonym Climacus. A more benign form of it
could be stated thus: nothing that we know can either establish or
disestablish the truth of Christian revelation. The relationship between knowledge and faith would thus be one of neutrality. The
twain would simply never meet. Whether or not Kierkegaard
accepts this, it is clear that Thomas Aquinas rejects it.

3. HISTORY AND FAITH[4]

Climacus argues this in the *Fragments* in terms of what we
should likely call the "problem of the historical Jesus." Kierke-

---

[4] Under the influence of Hegel, Kierkegaard sees philosophy not in terms of
classical metaphysics so much as in terms of history. In the preface to *The Philoso-*

gaard antedates the "problem," but he has things to say that are
extremely relevant to it.

The historical method, he suggests, is a technique meant to put
us into the position of eyewitnesses. So let us grant to historical
research success beyond its wildest dreams. Not only does it put
us into the shoes of an eyewitness; it makes of us a kind of com-
posite or ideal eyewitness such that we know the past even better
than individual witnesses of the past events in question. (Think
of the different eyewitness reports on even a fairly simple auto-
mobile accident.) Can such historical research enable us to decide
the truth about Jesus?

Well, were the contemporaries of Christ, all those who heard
and saw Him, compelled to accept that He was both human and
divine? Many saw and did not believe. Not all who believed were
in the front row, so to speak, and not everyone in the front row
believed. Whatever truths history puts us in possession of fall
short of those truths which characterize Christ as the Son of God:
Before Abraham was, I am. The Father and I are one . . . . Eyewitnesses, simply by dint of being eyewitnesses, did not grasp
those truths. If this is so, even the most successful application of
the historical method would put us in possession of truths *which
do not entail the distinctive and central truths — the mysteries —
of Christian faith.*

An Asymmetrical Relation

In this, Climacus is surely right. Not even such miracles as the
raising of Lazarus led all witnesses to accept Christ as the one He
claimed to be. What Climacus is less clear on is that there is an
asymmetrical relation between history and faith. While the historical, in the sense of what can be established by the historical

---

phy of History, Hegel says it is our religious duty not only to love God, but also
to know Him. And where can God be known? In history, which is the providential
unrolling of the divine plan. God, as the Lord of History, is grasped through Philosophical History. Thus the question is no longer what is the relation between nature
and God, but rather what is the relation between history and God.

method, does not entail the truth of Christianity, Christianity entails the truth of any number of historical claims. That a son was
born to Mary, the spouse of Joseph, in Bethlehem is a historical
claim which, in principle, is susceptible of being established or dis-
established by the historical method. If it were proved to be an
historical truth, this would not establish the divinity of Christ. *But
if it could be shown to be a false claim, the distinctive truths of
Christianity would also be disproved.* That is what I mean by asym-
metry. History cannot establish the truths of faith, but it could
disestablish them.

Thomas would express this in terms of what can be known of
God and what we believe of God. The truths that philosophers
come to know of God do not entail those truths called mysteries.
A successful proof that there is a God does not as such establish
that Jesus was human and divine. But of course if it could be
shown that the claim that there is a God is conceptually inco-
herent, if we came to know there is no God, this would destroy the
Christian belief that Jesus is human and divine. It is because of
this that the Catholic Church has always considered philosophy to
be of importance for the community of believers. It is, however,
important to understand that importance correctly.

The importance does not lie in this — and the phrase *preambles of faith* perhaps invites this misunderstanding — that in
order to become a believer I must first establish knowable truths
about God.[5] Philosophical knowledge about God does not entail
those truths about God that characterize Christian belief. In
Thomas's terminology, the preambles do not entail the mysteries.
But, because certain claims about the way things are, certain teach-
ings of philosophers, are such that, if they were true, Christianity
could not be true, the Church must concern Herself with philosophy. The believer could not of course consistently hold that the
opposite of what he believes is true in the sense that both his belief

    [5] In this regard, see Etienne Gilson, *Le philosophe et la théologie* (Paris:
Librarie Athème Fayard, 1960), especially "Les enfances théologiques," pp. 11–25.

and its opposite are true. The refusal to entertain this, far from being obscurantism, is an obvious instance of the most basic principle of rationality: "—(p.—p.)." Holding as he does that what has been revealed is true, he is committed in all consistency to the falsehood of what conflicts with it, or at least to the mere probability of the opposite.

At the end of *Fear and Trembling*, another of Kierkegaard's pseudonyms recalls the teaching of Heraclitus, the champion of flux, that one cannot step twice into the same river. Heraclitus had a disciple so enthusiastic that he went his master one better and declared that one cannot step even once into the same river! But far from increasing flux, this stops it dead. "Poor Heraclitus, to have had such a disciple." From Thomas's point of view, Climacus is somewhat in the position of that disciple of Heraclitus. From the truth that the mysteries of faith cannot be understood, he goes on to deny that anything about God can be known by human reason. Far from preserving the difference between faith and reason, this transforms faith into the enemy of reason, and it becomes difficult to understand why Kierkegaard wrote all those books.[6]

The Reasonableness of Faith

What I have said could create the impression that the believer always looks at natural reason and its products with suspicion, seeing in them a possible threat to faith's hegemony. There is no doubt that the deposit of faith must be cherished and guarded, and that bad reasons can create difficulties for the faith far beyond their intrinsic merits. But it is the mark of the believer that he holds to the unity of truth. What the human mind unaided can come to know must complement rather than conflict with what God has told us about Himself. Our minds are God's gift just as

---

[6] The answer to this, it seems to me, is that we should not identify the views expressed by pseudonyms with the views of Kierkegaard himself. It could be argued that Climacus's notion of an "acoustical illusion" produced when reason asserts that the faith is absurd is a version of natural theology. What is absurd is the spectacle of finite reason demanding that everything be clear to it.

faith is. There are those who speak of a twofold revelation: God speaks to us through the world, through His creatures, as well as through His Son. It makes no sense to think that God is giving us conflicting messages through these two sources.

Supernatural truth is above and beyond natural truth but is perfectly consistent with it. G. K. Chesterton, in his remarkable little book about Thomas Aquinas, sees this reconciliation, this complementarity of faith and reason as the heart of Thomas's achievement.[7] The history of the West would have been wholly different if Thomas had not bested the Latin Averroists.[8]

If Thomas is right and Scripture itself contains two kinds of truths about God, those knowable by natural reason — the preambles — and those beyond the grasp of human reason in this life — the mysteries — an argument can be fashioned for the reasonableness of accepting as true what one cannot presently know to be true. It would go like this. If some of the things God has revealed can be known to be true and thus intelligible, it is reasonable to accept everything that He has revealed as true and intelligible.

This is not of course an argument on behalf of the truth of any mystery of faith, say, the Incarnation; it is an argument on behalf of the reasonableness of accepting the mystery as true. The analogy with my student Yorick goes to this point — and can indeed be expanded to just about anyone with whom we deal daily. We trust one another, not blindly, but because others have generally proved trustworthy in the past. We distrust those who have generally proved untrustworthy in the past. This is reasonable in both

[7] Gilbert Keith Chesterton, *Saint Thomas Aquinas: The Dumb Ox* (New York: Doubleday Image Books, 1956). The book first appeared in 1933. Maisie Ward's account of the writing of this book taxes one's credulity, though there is no reason to doubt what she says (*G. K. Chesterton* [New York: Sheed & Ward, 1943]). If her account is so, it is even more remarkable that Chesterton dashed off a book which has been the admiration, and envy, of professional Thomists since it first appeared.

[8] Cf. my *Thomas Against the Averroists: On There Being Only One Intellect* (Lafayette, Indiana: Purdue University Press, 1993).

cases, even though in this instance our friend may betray us and our enemy befriend us. It is not part of our trusting one another that we think it is impossible for someone to act out of character. But one of the truths we believe about God is that He can neither deceive nor be deceived.

If everything that has been revealed were a mystery, if there were no link whatsoever between what we believe and what we know, it would be unreasonable to believe, and faith would not be a viable option for a rational creature.

4. The Logic of Conversion

I said earlier that most undergraduates respond in the negative to the question whether God's existence can be proved. They are not prompted by having examined particular proofs and finding them logically wanting: when the question is put to them they can not formulate any proof of their own or recount any of the traditional proofs. Is this just one more proof of the irrationality of the young, the failure of our educational system, the decline of the West, and so on? I don't think so. Of course I don't think it is a disproof of any of the things I just mentioned either. In my experience, the skepticism about proofs of God's existence derives from a sense of the limitations of proof.

After Johannes Climacus has rejected both natural theology and history as ways to grasp the nature of faith, he provides us with a better analogy. He invites us to consider the relation between ethics and faith.

One of the oldest and most persistent questions of moral philosophy has to do with the apparent inefficaciousness of reason. It is possible for us to know the good for human persons, to grasp that in which fulfillment and perfection for such beings as we are consists, and yet fail to exemplify this knowledge in our lives. It is easy to see why Kierkegaard turned to this analogy. Christians, those who live in Christendom, know what Christianity is. They know their Catechism, they know the Creed, they can quote from

Scripture, they are difficult to stump. Is having that kind of knowledge what it means to be a Christian? *Be ye doers of the word, and not hearers only.* When Plato asked if knowledge were virtue, he was drawing our attention to the problematic relation between what we might call moral lore, knowledge, information, and practice.

A distinction that emerges from reflection on this problem is that between changing one's mind and changing one's life. The former is done on the basis of knowledge, argument, information. What we didn't know before, we now know. And this can be moral knowledge, the somewhat melancholy knowledge that emerges from our failures and falls. Let us say that we come to see that certain circumstances are dangerous for us, that in such circumstances we are likely to fall into sin. Does knowing this entail that we will avoid such circumstances in the future? We all know the answer. Knowledge is not enough. But knowledge is not nothing. What we did not know before, we have come to know. Our minds have been changed, or furnished, or altered. But the acquisition of knowledge does not *suffice* for changing our lives.

Religious conversion, like moral conversion, is more than a matter of changing our minds. What precisely is the "more"? There are some who say that the basic spring of action is passion, not knowledge: knowledge is just an ambulance chase after our feelings, and our feelings are not a product of thinking. There is another possibility, one suggested by Cardinal Newman.

Already in the University Sermons delivered in St. Mary's Church in Oxford, Newman reflected on the relation of faith and reason, belief and knowing. We can see his thoughts clarifying as he returns to this theme, but it is in the *Apologia* that he exhibits what he came to see. *It is unreasonable to hold that 'reasonable' always means the same thing.* The model of mathematical argument is rightly given pride of place in the scale of arguments: logicians suggest that there is a kind of cadenza of arguments away from this pure kind. Aristotle took it to be the mark of an educated man that he knew the kind of argument a subject matter could provide. It is wrong to expect metaphors and similes from a mathematician; it is a mistake to think that geometric argumentation about what we ought to do is possible. From this we do not conclude that ethics is irrational; we ask what kind of reasoning is appropriate to its subject matter.

But 'ethics' is ambiguous. It can mean the sort of thinking we find in the *Nicomachean Ethics* and the second part of the *Summa theologiae*. Or it can mean the kind of thinking that goes on when I do this or that. The thought that is the soul of action is a thought guided by my passionate orientation to an end. It is not abstract and impersonal; it is concrete and the very expression of the acting person's character.

Faith is an acceptance of what God reveals as true, but the mind is moved to accept because the will is moved by grace. "*Nemo credit nisi volens,*" St. Augustine said. The response to God in faith is very much like the singular judgments we make as to what we ought to do here and now — our mind moves under the prompting of love.

If abstract arguments for the existence of God were thought to produce this conversion, it is no wonder that people think they are impossible. A sound argument for the existence of God can change our minds, but it is a mistake to expect that it will change our lives.

The analogy between our moral lives and faith yields other important results. Not least among them is the recognition that there are often appetitive obstacles to our applying moral truths we know. Indeed, our character can be such that we are indisposed even to listen at a level of generality to arguments on behalf of, say, chastity. In morals as in religion, we need eyes to see and ears to hear. Or, to repeat the delightful image Kierkegaard borrowed from Lichtenburg, if a monkey looks into the mirror of faith, no apostle looks out.

And so I return to the Memorial of Blaise Pascal. It is possible to take his contrast of the God of Abraham, Isaac, and Jacob with the God of the philosophers as pointing to the inadequacy of the latter compared to the former. Scripture conveys truths about God incomparably richer than those philosophers manage to achieve. But of course Pascal meant far more than this. He is recounting a religious experience, a conversion. He has turned with loving faith to God as the good to which his whole life is oriented. Next to this how pale, flat, and unprofitable must seem the tortured discourse of the philosopher. *Le coeur a ses raisons que la raison ne connait point.* Indeed. And it is the glory of Pascal, in a rationalist age, to have articulated and then underscored this truth. The heart has reasons that reason does not know. But this entails another truth that a Thomas Aquinas will never let us forget. The reasons of the heart, divorced from the reasons of reason, will soon lead us to absurdity. Kierkegaard called himself a corrective, not a norm. Pascal too is a corrective. Thomas Aquinas, or so it has always seemed to me, is the champion of the norm that Kierkegaard and Pascal were seeking to reestablish.

WESTMINSTER COLLEGE OF SALT LAKE CITY

Westminster College of Salt Lake City has been a vital part of Utah's history and educational heritage since 1875. The College was first known as the Presbyterian Preparatory School; later as the Salt Lake Collegiate Institute and Sheldon Jackson College; and, since 1902, as Westminster College. Continued growth and interest in the school and its goals prompted the College to become a four-year liberal arts institution in 1944.

Ownership of the College by the Presbyterian Church ended in 1974, and under the executive direction of a Board of Trustees Westminster became a fully independent, privately-funded, non-denominational liberal arts institution of higher learning.

Westminster College welcomes students of all religious and cultural backgrounds. Two thousand students representing thirty-seven states and twenty-three foreign countries are now enrolled at the College.

There are three schools within the College: the School of Arts and Sciences, the Bill and Vieve Gore School of Business, and the St. Mark's–Westminster School of Nursing and Health Science.

As an institution rooted in the Judaeo-Christian tradition, Westminster seeks to provide an environment that encourages and facilitates the intellectual, spiritual, cultural, and social growth of its students. To this end, the faculty and administration emphasize excellence in teaching, personalized instruction and advising, and flexible delivery systems to meet the needs of students of diverse ages and backgrounds.

Through a course of study that is both broad and intensive, the College expands each student's horizons beyond his or her chosen field of emphasis. In addition to preparing students for a career or profession, the goals of Westminster are to educate students to communicate intelligently; to develop in students an understanding of their social and natural environments; to encourage in students a critical appreciation of the world's literature, arts and religions; to make students aware of the ideas, attitudes, and events which have shaped the past and will shape the future; to foster in students originality and creativity; and to create in students the capacity for rigorous independent thought.

Westminster College of Salt Lake City is pleased and proud to present to the community the benefits of the Westminster Tanner–McMurrin Lectures on the History and Philosophy of Religion.

Edited and produced for Westminster College by
MCMURRIN–HENRIKSEN BOOKS.
Typeset in hot metal Intertype Garamond.
Printed by Publishers Press, Salt Lake City, and bound by
Roswell Book Binding, Phoenix, Arizona.